MISSING
the
POINT

MISSING
the
POINT

Why Acupuncturists Fail...
and What They Need to Know to Succeed

Lorne Brown
BSc, CPA, Dr.TCM, FABORM, CHt

Printed in the United States of America

First Printing, 2016

ISBN 978-0-9950551

Design and production: Toni Kenny
Cover illustration: BIGSTOCK/forestpath

Pro D Seminars Publishing
12106 Imperial Drive
Richmond BC V7E 6J5

www.prodseminars.com

DEDICATION

To my mother, for her unwavering support and love that gave me the courage to take risk and often leaps of faith while following my passion. I knew if I was not successful that she would be there to support me and provide me with a roof over my head until I landed on my feet. Fortunately, I never fell that far, but it sure gave me comfort knowing she always had my back. Thanks for believing in me.

I also want to express my gratitude to all of the people who read the draft versions of this book and provided me with their valuable feedback.

Special thank-yous to: Matthew Bauer, Debra Betts, Charles Buck, Claudia Citkovitz, Lorie Dechar, Felice Dunas, Yvonne Farrell, Susan Fox, Jeffrey Grossman, Leon Hammer, Lonny Jarrett, Njemile Jones, Kellie Krasovec, Christine Lang, Randine Lewis, Jane Lyttleton, Michael Max, Will Morris, Arya Nielsen, Sharon Weizenbaum, and Sabine Wilms.

CONTENTS

FOREWORD

Some years ago an extensive survey of acupuncturists found that only one in three graduates of an American acupuncture college was in practice after five years. An earlier study by the New England School of Acupuncture of their graduates found approximately the same statistics. Lorne Brown makes the case that an exquisite knowledge and performance of a skill such as acupuncture is an exercise in futility if it is not realized in a successful practice. He has written a book whose precepts, if followed reasonably well, would reverse those figures and allow for the realization of the goal of acupuncturists: to spend their life doing what they love, healing with Chinese medicine.

A Chinese medical practice is ordinarily built by one successful treatment, one satisfied patient at a time. Acupuncturists do not have hospitals where they were residents or have privileges referring patients. Dr. Brown presents a superb program that also builds character and the personal attributes necessary to an ongoing successful practice that obviates the dependence on hospital referrals and the self-defeating sense of entitlement.

Dr. Brown emphasizes attitude, first of all toward money, that reminds me of what my grandfather told me: "There is nothing wrong with money. It is the love of money that is the problem."

Read this book, learn and practice its suggestions, and then succeed and be fulfilled.

Leon I. Hammer, MD

Author of *Dragon Rises, Red Bird Flies: Psychology & Chinese Medicine* and *Chinese Pulse Diagnosis: A Contemporary Approach* and the founder of Dragon Rises College of Oriental Medicine www.comfoundation.org

How I Learned to Succeed

*If you don't change the direction you
are going, then you're likely to end
up where you're heading...*
—John Maxwell

What an incredible medicine we acupuncturists practice! It's a true blessing to get paid to do something you love that is also a service to your community. We are so fortunate to have this opportunity.

Unfortunately, for many it's a struggle.

I am the founder and clinical director of Acubalance Wellness Centre, the first Traditional Chinese Medicine (TCM) clinic in British Columbia dedicated to treating reproductive health and fertility issues. I started my practice in 2000, and by 2004 I was already hiring more practitioners to serve my waiting list of patients. At the time of this writing I have six associates—five who practice TCM and a naturopathic doctor—and the Acubalance model provides all of us with a comfortable living, as well as the knowledge that we're serving our community.

My other company, Healthy Seminars (which includes ProDSeminars.com, medigogy.com, and IFSymposium .com) offers online continuing education courses for TCM and functional medicine practitioners. Applying the principles in this book, Healthy Seminars, just like Acubalance, continues to enjoy rapid growth despite the fact that competition in the acupuncture online continuing education market has only increased.

I am not gifted or exceptionally smart. I don't have special talents that you, or any practitioner, lack.

I *was* blessed to learn a few key success principles early in life, which have allowed me to achieve some success. I attribute my success to the principles contained in this book and the following three important personal factors:

1. **Mentors**—My father, an entrepreneur in his own right, was my first mentor. He taught me that the individual, not the profession, determines success. He lived by the adage, "Choose a job you love, and you will never work a day in your life." That advice stuck with me and gave me the courage to leave my previous career as a chartered professional accountant (CPA) and follow my passion to study Chinese medicine. I have been fortunate to have other mentors, too—business mentors in my previous career, and now doctor mentors such as Randine Lewis, author of *The Infertility Cure*, to support my growth as a Chinese medicine practitioner.

2. **Self-investment**—Truly successful people never stop learning. One of my mottos is to live like you

will die tomorrow; learn like you will live forever. So I constantly invest in myself through books, educational programs, and coaching. I invest more than $1,000 a year (some years it has been more than $10,000) in myself. I contribute much of my success to the investments I have made in continued professional development and personal growth.

3. **Professional credentials**—In addition to being a doctor of TCM, I am a chartered professional accountant and previously worked as a controller for one of the Ocean Spray cranberry farms in Richmond, British Columbia. Accounting may seem like a far cry from TCM, but I like to joke that they are both about creating balance—as an accountant I would balance your debits and credits and as a Chinese medicine practitioner I balance your yin and yang. Joking aside, I gained invaluable experience and knowledge of what allows a business to succeed (and, equally important, fail) through auditing a diverse list of business clients.

I realize that not everyone has been fortunate to have the mentors I have had, and most of you don't have a background as a CPA. However, that doesn't mean you lack that business sense to succeed. We all have life experiences we can apply to our Chinese medicine practice. We've invested thousands of hours and tens of thousands of dollars in training. There isn't a single one of us who is not passionately dedicated to helping others.

And if math doesn't make a bit of sense to you, you have unique talents that I lack.

Unfortunately, many acupuncturists struggle to get by, because although they possess the skill and commitment to serve, they lack the knowledge of how to build and maintain a sustainable practice. All too often I hear stories about acupuncturists taking part-time jobs to make ends meet or quitting their practice to take on a full-time job elsewhere that pays the bills.

Why do acupuncturists fail? Acupuncturists fail because they run small businesses and it is common for small businesses to fail. It is not isolated to acupuncturists needing to find new jobs or take on part-time work. The same is true for naturopaths and other individuals who go to work for themselves. Running a small business brings with it challenges. To ignore or be in denial that you run a small business just increases your risk of failing.

I hope *Missing the Point* will inspire you and motivate you to take steps to build your dream practice. Everyone reading this book is at his or her own spot on the path to success, so whether you're just starting out or have been practicing for decades, or whether you're trying to increase patient volume or are already in a place of abundance, I hope you'll incorporate a few of the business pearls of wisdom contained in this book to help you reach your full potential and take advantage of all the opportunities that await you.

It only takes a few continuous action steps to fill your schedule with clients. The principles I'm sharing with you here have worked for both Acubalance and Pro D Seminars, as well as for my colleagues who sought me out for practice-building advice. I'm confident the principles in this book will give you the edge to create a thriving medical practice with *integrity*. Through these principles, you will be rewarded both financially and spiritually, increasing your client base, profits, and contribution to the world.

At the same time, remember that anything of real value takes time to build. Nolan Bushnell, founder of Atari and Chuck E. Cheese's, once said: "Everyone who's ever taken a shower knows what an idea is. It's the person who gets out of the shower, dries off, and does something about it that makes a difference." The difference comes down to sustained effort, even when it feels fruitless.

So although this is simple, it's not easy. You don't need a Mensa-level IQ or special schooling, but you do need a willingness to work and keep working.

Please take five minutes to focus in the moment and assess where you are today and where you want to be one, three, five, and ten years from now. Then use the concepts from this book to start planting the seeds of your vision to reap the rewards of harvest in your future.

Really, all the actions needed to be successful are found in chapter 17, but they are so simple and obvious that without reading the first sixteen chapters, they are at risk of being dismissed.

So I recommend reading this book at least twice and really taking the time to study the principles in parts I and II so that you fully understand them all. If something needs clarification, please send me an e-mail at success@ ProDSeminars.com. Once you feel confident that you truly grasp the essence of this book, then start implementing the actions in part III, and especially chapter 17.

And remember, like it or not, you are in business.

Lorne Brown
BSc, CPA, Dr.TCM, FABORM, CHt

What I Wish They Taught Us in Chinese Medicine School: Like It or Not, You're a Small-Business Owner!

The entrepreneur always searches for change, responds to it, and exploits it as an opportunity.
—PETER DRUCKER

Most of us chose acupuncture because we wanted to help people. Running a business was not really on our radar. We naïvely imagined that all we needed to do was learn the medicine well, rent a room, put up a shingle announcing our practice, launch our name into cyberspace with a basic website, and watch the patients flock to our clinic door.

We were not prepared for the business side of the practice. We invested years of our lives and tens of thousands of dollars becoming well-trained, licensed

Chinese medicine practitioners, but as soon as we set up shop and started offering services for money, we were rudely awakened to realities such as accounting, marketing, hiring staff, and staying ahead of government forms and taxes. These skills were not adequately taught in our training, but they are as integral to a successful Chinese medicine practice as is our healing knowledge and skill.

Actually, that's not quite true. I would argue that those entrepreneurial skills are *more* integral to a busy TCM practice.

Too many TCM practitioners operate under the myth that to have a thriving practice, you must be a scholar and a clinically skilled master of Chinese medicine. But *your clinical skills have little bearing on how busy you are or how much you can charge for your services.* Why? Because patients cannot tell the difference between a good acupuncture/herbal prescription from a poor one.

That's an important point, and one that most practitioners are in denial about, so I'm going to say it again: *Patients cannot tell the difference between a good acupuncture/herbal prescription and a bad one.* Your patients are not experts in Chinese medicine, so they cannot judge your treatments. Though the quality of the work might affect retention and word of mouth, your patients choose their acupuncture practitioner based on a variety of *emotional, financial,* and *interpersonal* factors that are often independent of any clinical factors. So if you want to help as many people as possible and receive fair payment for your valuable work, you have to know how to connect with patients on emotional, financial, and interpersonal levels.

Many TCM practitioners find it challenging to meld the identities of "businessperson" and "health-care provider." Some have a mental block to financial success—perceiving money as the root of all evil—while others lack the work ethic required to succeed. But hopefully once you acknowledge that you are the CEO, marketing manager, accountant, healer, counselor, and janitor of your business, your perception will change.

Practitioners who reject their role as business owners experience meager earnings and endless amounts of frustration, whereas if you do accept that your roles as businessperson and healer are mutually dependent (just like the laws of yin and yang), then you can create a future where the sky is the limit.

You control your destiny and the success of your acupuncture practice. And one day, instead of wondering where it all went wrong, you'll marvel at all the people you've been able to help and who have happily paid you for the improved quality of life you helped them create.

❧ PUT IT INTO PRACTICE ❧

I created this book for health-care providers. The success principles contained in this book apply to any small business, but I had in mind acupuncturists and other individuals providing medical healing to our communities. When I set out to write *Missing the Point*, my goal was to create short but impactful chapters. I have added at the end of each chapter a section called "Putting It into Practice." Having an idea and good intention is the first step; however, to manifest success in your life requires action, too. The "Putting It into Action" will help you start the process of taking action.

Part I
The Chi (Qi) of a Successful Practice

1
It Starts with Attitude

Nothing can stop the man with the right mental attitude from achieving his goal; nothing on earth can help the man with the wrong mental attitude.

—THOMAS JEFFERSON

Attitude is the foundation on which everything is built. You've no doubt heard of the law of attraction—the notion that you acquire that which you ask for; that you attract back to you the energy you put out it into the world. Which means that attitude is a self-fulfilling prophecy; if you're struggling financially, it's because deep down you're putting into the universe a vibration consistent with financial struggles.

With a background as a clinical hypnotherapist, my training and experience has taught me two indisputable truths:

1. Your actions inevitably follow your beliefs.
2. When there is a conflict between your heart

(subconscious) and your brain (conscious desires), your heart always wins.

This is bad news for most acupuncturists, because in our culture we're trained—if not explicitly, then through acquiring the attitudes of our peers—to believe that money is inherently evil. We're taught that either we prioritize the spiritual aspect of healing and helping, or we make money. We can never do both. And so we revile the "world's curse" and vilify those who have money; we revel in our own altruism and martyr ourselves in the process.

The thing is, it's not true. The *individual* determines if money is used for good or evil. Money is not inherently evil. It is just chi (qi). It is the energetic exchange between practitioner and patient. Consider: If you won $40 million today, would you buy a bigger house? A nicer car? A bigger practice? Would you travel? Maybe you would, maybe you wouldn't, but look deeper into the material items that spring to mind and consider what these things represent: safety and security, freedom, comfort, status and influence, and the ability to help others.

Many of us chose the Chinese healing profession to be of service to others because service brings us happiness. So if everything you could do and buy with that $40 million is a means for you to achieve happiness, and your happiness rests in serving others, then that money gets to be used to that end.

So while money can't buy true happiness, your capacity to earn it can be a measurement of your ability to serve others. When you have great service at a restaurant, you don't resent giving the server a larger tip—you give that money freely as an acknowledgment of the service she's provided. And your server doesn't feel guilty for taking it, either, because you gave it willingly and are acknowledging her for a job well done. So why feel guilty when receiving money from patients? You're not forcing them to see you. You are simply offering a service, for which they acknowledge the value. Furthermore, placing a healthy value on your skills and making sure you get paid what you are worth are the means to building your practice so that you can reach more people: the more you earn from your business, the more you can afford to be generous in other ways and pay it forward. It is absolutely possible to help people while making a great living without abandoning your integrity or your ethics.

Your attitude toward this shift in perspective is the key. If you cringe when money hits your palm or anytime you see a fancy watch, that's a pretty good indicator you are repelling money by telling the universe that you don't want it. You can't expect to attract the very thing you want or need if you are putting out negative vibes against it into the ether. If the conscious (wants) and the subconscious (deep-seated beliefs) are ever in conflict, the subconscious always wins in the end. So if your mind says, "I want money," but your heart says, "Money is evil," that subconscious belief will sabotage the validity of earning that money, even though it's necessary to your practice and your life.

So the first, most important step is to shift your attitude and beliefs. Only then will it make a consistent positive difference. One of my mentors, a multidisciplinary counselor Gila Golub, reminds me to live consciously and to get out of my story by saying "Your thoughts create your reality, but only 100 percent of the time." And the deeper meaning of this quote is that your thoughts about your reality create your experience of that reality.

⤙ PUT IT INTO PRACTICE ⤚

Gauge Your Attitude

Answer the following questions, *and be honest*:
- Do you feel guilty or uncomfortable accepting payments from your patients?
- Does the energy of money align with your intentions for your life and practice?
- Do you believe money is evil?
- How often do you say, "I can't afford it" or "It's too expensive"?
- When you see signs of opulence—large houses, fancy cars, or people with money—do you tend to get uncomfortable, judgmental, irritable, resentful, embarrassed, or have some other kind of negative thought or emotion?

If your answers highlight for you a negative relationship with financial success—congratulations! You have uncovered an underlying cause to your inability to having it all. Now you can work on changing your attitude toward money!

Make the Conscious Unconscious

Remember, in a conflict between the conscious and subconscious, the subconscious always wins. Your actions over the long term are aligned with your beliefs and not your conscious desires. So once you've made the conscious choice to welcome abundance into your life, you'll need to move that attitude into your subconscious.

How do you do this? The first step is identifying those underlying beliefs that may be self-sabotaging your success. When you experience negative emotions, take some time to reflect by breathing into the physical sensations rather than avoiding the uncomfortable feeling. Allow yourself to be curious while you continue to search for a deep-seated belief that is no longer serving your best interest now.

I also recommend seeking out an experienced clinical hypnotherapist, as a skilled practitioner can assist you in uncovering subconscious beliefs and reprogramming them to serve you better. I wrote this book to help you incorporate the attitudes and habits of successful people so that you too can enjoy a life of joy and financial abundance. By reading this book you will be able to incorporate these concepts and adopt the attitudes of successful people.

2
Compound Effect—
Persistence Is Key

Fall seven times and stand up eight.
—JAPANESE PROVERB

In *The Compound Effect,* author Darren Hardy poses an interesting question: Would you rather have $3 million instantly, or a penny that doubles every day for thirty days? Many people opt for the instant gratification and take the $3 million right away. But they don't understand what Hardy knows—the power of the compounding principal.

Let's say you choose the $3 million as you want the instant life of luxury, and I take the penny that doubles every day for thirty days because I have read this book and I understand how slow-and-steady wins the race when it comes to the compound effect.

By the tenth day, while you are vacationing in Hawaii, I have earned a grand total of ten dollars. Hmm. Not such an auspicious start for me, is it? By the twentieth day, I have accumulated only $10,000. I am still plugging away and you have not worked a day in almost three weeks.

Even twenty-eight days in, I have not quite reached the $3 million you received on day one. But by the thirtieth day, my earnings have leapt to over $10 million—more than triple what you got for taking the $3 million all at once! The takeaway here is that *the smallest actions, performed consistently, often produce enormous results.*

But there's another fundamental truth at play here, too: if you want to be successful, you have to put the hours in consistently, daily, and over time.

We've always known that practice makes perfect, yet people continue to fall for the get-rich-quick schemes that don't actually work. We covet those overnight success stories, even though every one of them was years or even decades in the making.

Achieving success is simple but not easy because it takes sustained effort, persistence, and dedication. You have to work every day. If you implement a strategy but fail to do so consistently, you'll only be left with disappointment; this is why only a few acupuncturists make over $75,000 before taxes a year, and even fewer make over $200,000. But if you persevere through the weeks, months, and years, you will achieve real success.

Malcolm Gladwell's excellent book *Outliers: The Story of Success* says it takes a minimum of ten thousand hours of practice for a person to achieve mastery in any activity or discipline. One of the examples he uses in his book is Bill Gates—the man many consider to have lucked into discovering the home computer. What most people don't know is that Bill Gates began studying the nascent computer technology that existed when he was a teenager.

Night after night, he snuck into the computer lab and spent hours there alone, mastering something he loved so much he was driven to understand it, to create with it. He put in 9,999 hours before the ten thousandth hour that the world perceived as his meteoric rise to success.

The process of success is small-scale, constant, and often overlooked. I liken it to an old-fashioned well, the kind with a hand pump. You might pump the handle a hundred times before you see any water. But it is that hundredth pump that everyone notices. No one sees the ninety-nine times you doggedly pumped the handle without results.

With that in mind, focus on showing up every day, even when you may not want to. Let the *passion* you feel for the TCM part of your practice inspire you to find satisfaction in all the other roles your small business demands you to play every day.

Self-promotion, educating the public about the medicine you practice and about you as a professional who practices the medicine, is a great example of the kind of work you have to keep putting in even when you don't see an immediate, obvious benefit. Many practitioners mistakenly believe that self-promotion is the enemy of ability. They imagine that if they are good at what they do, people will just find them. They even have a sense that self-promotion is somehow unethical—another of the limiting beliefs many TCM practitioners have.

Remember, we are medical professionals, not hucksters selling swampland. We offer a real service that tangibly benefits the lives of our patients. Letting people know that such a service is available, that we exist, isn't just good for business, it's good for the patients searching for someone to address their health concerns.

But we can't just buy a few ads, throw up a website, and call it a day. Part of self-promotion is building a reputation as an expert; sharing your knowledge with others by consistently writing articles or blogs for publications, holding public talks, or even developing your own web presence to establish you as an authority in your field. (We'll talk about this later on in the book.) One blog, one video, or one lecture will not cement your reputation, but over time, those things will add up to a consistent body of work, bringing you closer and closer to your ten thousand hours. People who research you and find a long track record of intelligent commentary on your practice will be much more likely to consider you a reliable source. And then one day, on that hundredth pump, you will "suddenly" be a respected and sought-after figure in your field, and then momentum will be on your side and water will flow from your well with every continued stroke.

Your intention behind this level of dedication is what creates the prosperous reality of your dream practice, helps the people who need you, and expands your influence beyond the walls of your treatment room.

⊰⊱ PUT IT INTO PRACTICE ⊰⊱

First, keep showing up daily. Maintain the effort. Perseverance is key. Never give up your goal, whatever it may be.

Second, find something that you know will make a difference for growing your practice, but that you haven't done or have stopped doing. Why did you stop doing it? What could you do that you would enjoy doing for a while, even if it doesn't show immediate results? Nobody's saying that you have to suffer through every moment of self-promotion, but if you like writing articles, you can set up a blog; if you're an extrovert, you can go to networking meetings; if you like teaching, you can set up a free class, et cetera. The more you enjoy it, the more likely you are to stick with it, which is key, because it's the sticking with it (compound effect) that produces the results.

3
Learn to Attract Patients

*The most expensive piece of real estate
is the six inches between your right and
left ear. It's what you create in that area
that determines your wealth. We are
only really limited by our mind.*
—DOLF DE ROOS

The "Pro D" in my online company name, Pro D Seminars, stands for professional development, which is the term used by other professionals for continuing education. Since its inception in 2005, the tagline has been *Knowledge—Confidence—Success*. This tagline speaks to one of the most fundamental truths of successful entrepreneurs: always protect your confidence. Success is dependent on your confidence and belief in what you are doing, and the best way to boost your confidence is through deepening knowledge.

It took me a few years to see this pattern, but once I did, it became obvious. For a lot of practitioners, continuing education is just a necessary evil to keep their licenses current. Even those who have a positive context for it rarely see it as much more than "making sure their knowledge is up to date," which is the reason licensing bodies require continuing education in the first place. But it actually goes much deeper than that. *By investing in yourself through continual study, you will actually attract more patients to your practice.*

People crave certainty, especially from their medical professionals. They come to you because they are hurting and need help. They are already nervous enough for the both of you. Your job is to be a source of knowledge, stability, and comfort. Confidence is as tangible as the wind—we cannot see it, but we certainly feel it. It's clear when someone is sure of him- or herself, and it's equally clear when a person is filled with self-doubt. So when a patient comes into your practice, even though they can't tell if you're above or below average at what you do, they *can* tell if you doubt yourself—and it will sour them on your practice.

Unfortunately, one of the biggest issues practitioners of acupuncture (as well as other forms of complementary and alternative medicines) have to face is an ingrained feeling of inadequacy. The allopathic medical community is slow to recognize our value, which means that if we don't keep building up our confidence, we'll fall into a rut.

Investing in yourself through continued study not only protects your confidence but also helps attract clients. Consider the following letter, which I received from an acupuncturist who took some pregnancy courses through Pro D Seminars:

Dear Lorne,

On Sunday, I finished two courses on pregnancy. I had just finished printing out my CEUs when I got a call. "I know this is Sunday, but my baby is overdue, and any help you might be able to give me would be great . . ." That same week, a second woman called up with a cracked rib from the baby. She was very anxious about the birth, and I was able to calm her down and put in ear seeds. The second woman I saw said she is going to recommend me to two of her pregnant friends.

Yours,
Nancy, LAc

I get this kind of feedback all the time. I'm sure you've even noticed it yourself: you take a weekend workshop or online course, and almost immediately you start getting calls to treat the exact condition for which you just completed the course work.

Quite simply, this is just the law of attraction at work. As your knowledge deepens, so does your belief and confidence in the effectiveness of the medicine. This confidence acts like an amplifier to the intention you put out into the universe, which then becomes a beacon attracting patients to your practice.

This universal dynamic is so simple, it is at risk of being dismissed, so I'm going to say it again: knowledge strengthens your confidence, which amplifies the intention you send out into the ether and acts as a beacon attracting back to you what you put out. It's that simple.

Learning every day and taking advantage of opportunities

to hone your craft is like putting money in the bank. It builds the energy that magnetizes more. Learning builds more confidence, more empathy, and more opportunities. Developing and deepening your own skill set assures you, your patients, and the world that you have something to be confident about.

When I decided to specialize in reproductive health, I didn't just take one weekend course and then call it a good day. I devoted my time to study and ongoing reading of research in this area. I took as many continuing education classes as I could find on the topic. I participate daily in reading and discussing case studies on the American Board of Oriental Reproductive Medicine (ABORM) private group and continue to take annually professional development classes about my specialty. My point is you cannot become an expert from a weekend workshop, and it takes a lifetime of study and dedication. I make sure I understand issues around reproduction and fertility not only from a Chinese medicine standpoint but in terms of Western medicine as well. I familiarize myself with the leading experts in the field and, in many cases, have corresponded or met with them.

Over the years, I have developed a network of relevant contacts in all sorts of disciplines. I know their histories, their strengths and weaknesses, and the types of patients they prefer.

This network, combined with my understanding of my own strengths and limitations as a TCM practitioner, makes me a very useful resource to both patients and other providers. When patients have a question about any reproductive problem, I am confident that I can answer it or point them to the best resource who can. I am also confident that I can tailor a program of treatment to their unique needs and that I will not be completely stumped by a challenging or unconventional case. Even more, I am confident that if I cannot treat them personally, I can direct them to someone more appropriate. And likewise, since other providers know this about me, if they have a patient that I'd be a better fit to treat, many of them will send that patient to me.

When it comes to investing in your education, there is no such thing as wasted effort. Everything is qi. You— your knowledge, intuition, and presence—are the most valuable commodity you offer to others. Every class, dollar, or hour you spend deepens who you are, increases qi, and brings you an immeasurable return on your investment. Remember, live like you will die tomorrow but *learn like you will live forever.*

⚘ PUT IT INTO PRACTICE ⚘

Take the next step and strengthen your confidence by deepening your knowledge in your medicine. Schedule learning time for a minimum of three hours per week for the next six weeks, through reading books and articles and taking classes. Make sure to choose topics that are of interest to you. If the material does not inspire and motivate you, then it is not likely that it is amplifying the intention you are sending out to the universe to make you a magnet of attraction. You actually have to *feel* inspired from the learning for it to attract patients.

4

Focus on Return on Investment

Our intentions create our reality.
—Dr. Wayne W. Dyer

Return on investment (ROI) is a business/finance term describing the amount of profit you receive for the money you put in. If you invest ten dollars and receive eleven dollars back (for a dollar profit), your ROI is 10 percent.

Though the distinction is simple, for many people it's quite a challenge to put it into practice, because they let themselves get hung up on the cost. Successful people, however, evaluate the ROI, and if the return looks promising, they find a way to afford the investment.

With that in mind, any opportunity you have to invest in your practice—whether it's through continuing education, marketing, or hiring new employees—should be done working backward, starting with how much you can gain long term from the expenditure.

Consider this example: There is an excellent online course for treating infertility with Chinese medicine. It's available for $499 and provides 19 CEU/PDAs. Using "poor man's thinking," you might grumble about the cost and decide that it's "too expensive." But if you look at it with a focus on the ROI, you might wonder, "Okay, what will I make in return for taking this course? What kind of patients will I be able to treat more confidently having taken this course? It turns out that the average infertility patient will come for three months for one or two acupuncture treatments per week, totaling 12–24 sessions; a woman undergoing in vitro fertilization (IVF) may also come for acupuncture on her embryo transfer day. Assuming you charge $80 per visit, you'll receive $960 to $1,920 per patient plus an additional $160 to $500 for the acupuncture treatment on embryo transfer day, if she goes through an IVF.

From this standpoint, the $499 for the course is an excellent investment. You only need to enroll one new fertility patient to make back double what you paid for the course. You also deepen your knowledge, which, as we learned in the last chapter, increases your confidence that will strengthen the intention you put out into the ether to attract more fertility patients.

Notice that I'm not telling you to just blindly go out and spend money arbitrarily. I would not trade a ten-dollar bill for a five-dollar bill.

But by the same token, I challenge you to give up the phrase "That's too expensive." When we truly want something of value, we find a way to afford it. The question is how important is it to you to have it? If your attitude is "That's too expensive," your limited way of thinking robs you of potential future income. Remember, attitude is everything, and this is just one of those phrases that reinforces the poverty mentality of your subconscious.

So instead of focusing on what something costs, focus instead on the future earning you will get in return from that investment. Focus on how you will benefit and how much you will earn from your investments before deciding if the cost is reasonable for the ROI.

A gentle reminder that you chose this field so that you could help people by being of service and satisfying your passions and personal interest. I have never been initially motivated to choose projects based on money. The financial return does play into my final decision but not during the early stages of my decision making. I suspend the money part while keeping my entrepreneurial spirit in mind as I look to fill a need and create value for others. I check in with myself to make sure it will satisfy my interest and passions. Will it be enjoyable and a positive experience so that even if it is not financially rewarding, it will be rewarding in other areas of my life? Like you, I do not own a money tree or have a trust fund, so I need to earn income to enjoy the freedom and comfort I want in my life and to support causes that are important to me. So I do an ROI check before I move forward, but I wanted to let you know that I think the ordering is important when making decisions.

✎ PUT IT INTO PRACTICE ✎

The next time you find yourself saying, "That's too expensive," stop yourself and change your focus from the cost to the ROI. Ask yourself, "Over the next one to three years, how much will I gain in return from investing today?" If the ROI is worth it and allows you to help more people and have more satisfaction in life, then go for it.

5

Avoid the Destructive Entitlement Syndrome

*Character—the willingness to accept
responsibility for one's own life—is the
source from which self-respect springs.*
—Joan Didion

You already know how important attitude is. It affects your thinking, your actions, and the way you are perceived by others. Sadly, an entire generation in North America has grown up with an attitude that they deserve privilege and benefits without putting in the effort to earn them. At some point, the American dream mutated, and the Land of Opportunity became the Land of Entitlement.

Remember the Janet Jackson song "What Have You Done for Me Lately"? That's what this syndrome reminds me of. If you have this entitlement attitude—you believe that the world owes you something, that people should act a certain way toward you, or that some association or governing body is supposed to help you out—then there's unfortunately very little I can do for you. This attitude is the antithesis to the entrepreneurial spirit and certain to keep you from being successful.

In my lectures, I share two important tenets that are key to entrepreneurial success. The second of those I'll talk about in chapter 7. The first is this: *I depend entirely on my own abilities for financial security and freedom.* I do not expect the government, my association, or my regulatory body to support, take care of, or provide for me. Basically, I do not feel entitled to anything.

Each one of us deserves the *opportunity* to be successful, but we are not, by any means, owed that success. I am not aware of anyone achieving great things without putting in years of consistent effort. My father worked for every bit of success he now enjoys. When things were difficult and did not work out as expected, he increased his efforts. He worked harder, he thought creatively, and he never quit because he believed he was ultimately responsible for himself and his life.

It is not bad or wrong to want more, either in your practice or your personal life. Ambition is not entitlement—in fact, I encourage you to strive for a greater reach, more clients, better clinical results, increased press, and more financial freedom. What I am against is sitting on our hands, complaining about how life is not fair—or worse, spending energy being jealous of those who have what you want.

So avoid the entitlement attitude. Nobody owes you anything, and your associations are not going to save you, either. Entitlement turns you into a victim, blaming others for your shortcomings and preventing you from taking action to create your own success.

I would recommend you avoid hiring and working with people who have entitlement syndrome, too, as admin staff and associates with a sense of entitlement can be toxic to your practice. For example, I tend not to hire associates who just graduated from TCM school, opting instead to look for people who have been in practice for two years or longer. This is not about being "green" to practice—if you have a willingness to learn, then you can be mentored—it's because after two years they have had a reality check about the challenges of operating a practice in the real world and hopefully have lost that sense of entitlement.

Remember, entrepreneurs depend entirely on their own abilities for economic security and expect opportunity in life after having created value for others. This is the attitude necessary to achieve your dreams. Unfortunately, if you have entitlement syndrome, you probably do not even know it.

✤ PUT IT INTO PRACTICE ✤

I do not know how to cure a person plagued with entitlement syndrome. It is rampant in our society and possibly the demise of our economy.

I do suggest, as I said above, that you avoid hiring people who expect entitlements, whether for an admin position or an associate in your clinic. If they ask questions like "Do I have to work weekends?" or "Am I expected to do x, y, or z?" or blame others for their lack of successes or speak poorly of past employers, then these red flags may indicate they have entitlement syndrome.

Conversely, if someone demonstrates time after time that they are self-motivated and create value, make sure to pay them fairly and let them know you value them. People who lack entitlement are less demanding by nature, and you are at risk for taking them for granted and not acknowledging them properly. These individuals are gems and are hard to find, so when you do find them, hold on to them.

6

Patient-centric vs. Doctor-centric

If you were to ask a thousand acupuncturists whether their practice is patient centered, the vast majority would no doubt give you a resounding yes. Ask them what makes them patient centered, they may have a harder time answering—but even if they were able to answer that question, it would probably be a vague and unspecific response such as "We put the patient first," for example.

Patient-centered care means constantly putting yourself in the patient's shoes. Consider for a moment the images on your website and marketing materials. Do you have images of people receiving acupuncture with close-ups of needles and burning moxa?

This is the perfect example of the difference between a doctor-centered and a patient-centered approach to your promotional images. As acupuncturists, pictures of needles inserted in a person's back, smoking moxa, and red marks left behind from cupping are appealing to us. We are passionate about acupuncture and are not turned off by the thought of being "needled" at all. But the vast majority of people have a fear of needles. To them, those images aren't relaxing at all. They can be anxiety producing and repulsive. Dentistry is a great example. Have you ever seen a dentist's advertisement contain pictures of a large needle puncturing the gum for freezing or a drill digging into a tooth to remove a cavity? Obviously not. Instead, dentists use pleasant photos of adults and children looking happy, displaying perfectly straight white teeth and a beautiful smile. To borrow from the travel industry: sell Paris, not the airplane.

Remember, patients aren't coming to you for acupuncture; they're coming to you for a solution to their problems. If your website is full of acupuncture pictures, then you are not fully putting yourself in your prospective patients' shoes, and this may be costing you new patients.

––––

Listen to Your Patients

Patient-centered care also means actively listening attentively and patiently while carefully communicating in a manner so that your patient feels heard and imbued with hope. People commit to practitioners whom they trust and believe care about their well-being. Allowing your patients to feel heard and listened to is essential in building that trust; it communicates in a nonverbal way that you care about them.

Many practitioners make the mistake of overwhelming their patients with too much information or presenting them with too many services that do not directly apply. As healers, we are passionate about our work and we've worked hard to become knowledgeable experts in our field, so it's natural for us to get excited about techniques, methods, and services we offer. But our patients come for particular solutions and they may not share our enthusiasm for our medicine.

If patients come into your clinic struggling with chronic headaches, all they want or need to know from you is that you can confidently and effectively relieve their headaches. Your job is to learn what their expectations are for coming to see you. Are they looking for 100 percent relief of symptoms or simply a reduction in intensity and frequency? What would success look like for them?

It might seem obvious that you should ask a patient why they are coming to see you, but I've seen many practitioners skip that step and simply make an assumption. More often than not, this is to the practitioner's detriment. A colleague made this unfortunate mistake when a very overweight woman came into his practice for knee pain. Because of the woman's physical appearance, he assumed that she wanted help with weight loss, too. While acupuncture is frequently used for that purpose, his failure to respectfully confirm his assumption with the patient resulted in him offending her deeply. As it turned out, she was hoping to get relief for her knee pain only and did not see her weight as an issue. Since her weight was never discussed, she was insulted when he included weight loss in her treatment plan. If he'd taken the time to discuss this with his patient (introducing the idea of weight loss to take pressure off her knee), the conversation around the topic of her weight could have occurred naturally, allowing her to feel heard and express her personal view. Instead, he insulted her and lost a patient he could have helped—and anyone she would have referred.

Listening is yin. Talking is yang. If you spend your appointment time talking about all the services you offer, then you are not listening enough and can miss having your patients tell you precisely what they need from you to become a committed patient. If you take the time to really listen to your patients, you will be able to pick out the services you provide that can offer solutions to their problems. Listening includes not imposing your worldview or trying to "fix" the patient but being truly of service only to the patient, having our own ego step out of the way. The moral of the story: talk less, listen more, and listen first before speaking.

✦ PUT IT INTO PRACTICE ✦

Great salespeople do not begin a sales call by telling you about every product and service they offer. Instead, they ask you questions, listen for you to tell them the solution you are looking for, and then present the service or product that fits the solution you described. This lets them (1) save time talking to people who don't actually want what they have to offer, and (2) avoid pitching a buffet of options so that they can figure out what's most important to the client and then address those concerns specifically.

In other words, great salespeople spend most of their time listening. And like it or not, you are in sales—selling health and acupuncture services. So pay attention to how much you are speaking during each session and focus on keeping your talking to less than 50 percent compared to your patients' talking time.

I always start every initial consult by taking a few minutes to understand my patient's short- and long-term expectations of me. Asking about their expectations allows me to get into the listening mode and practice patient-centered care, and your patients begin their session feeling heard right from the start. Some of the questions I ask include:

- What are your expectations for your first visit today?
- What are your expectations for your course of treatment?
- What would you like to get out of our consultation today? Are you expecting an acupuncture treatment during this first session?

However, I want to know my patients' expectations not just at the first visit but at every visit. That way I can focus on patient-centered care 100 percent of the time. So at every visit I invite you to ask them their expectations, and be comfortable with any silence as your patients take a moment to reflect before answering.

And then (and here is the key) listen closely to the answers they give you.

7
Create Value and Profit Will Follow

Strive not to be a success,
but rather to be of value.
—ALBERT EINSTEIN

I only expect opportunities in life and to be paid after creating value for others. This attitude—which pushes me to excel and constantly improve my service to my patients—has been crucial to my success.

I know as an acupuncturist, you value your service. And you have invested a lot of time and money to treat people effectively and safely. But your patients aren't interested in paying off your school debts. For consumers to depart with their hard-earned cash, they need to see the value *for them.*

Think, for a moment, about who you typically perceive as an entrepreneur. It's probably an innovator of some kind, right? Steve Jobs or Mark Zuckerberg or Larry Page, who created extraordinary products, did it better than anyone else, and had people lining up to buy them or signing up by the millions to use them.

While you may not be reinventing the wheel or creating new acupuncture techniques, there's a lot to be learned from these individuals. They look at the world, the market, or a product and see it not just for what it is, but for everything it could be. They're constantly looking for ways to make things better, be it faster, cheaper, or more feature-rich. Google is constantly updating its algorithms and adding new services; a new version or upgrade of the iPhone comes out every year.

In other words, they are all looking for ways to provide value. Most people don't throw their money around indiscriminately, but if they really see the value in a product or service, they'll pay for that value.

So if you want to draw people to you, then you have to give them a good reason to come. Remember the early 2000s when you would wait to get a new cell phone until you could get the "free upgrade" that came with renewing your service contract? In those days, no one would ever think of replacing her cell phone until she could get that bonus. Today, many of us spend a lot of money on a new smartphone every year or two, even though the one we have still works. We went from never paying for a cell phone to paying for a new one almost every year. Why? Because we value having the most updated features a new smartphone provides.

Fees Are Tied to Deliverables

You do not get paid for working harder. You get paid for

creating value for others. Think about this for a moment. If we were sitting at opposite ends of a lecture hall and I offered you a ten-dollar bill in exchange for your twenty, all I'd get is a confused look. You might ask, "What else am I getting?" because we're so programmed to think in these terms that an exchange like that doesn't even make sense. And in this case it doesn't. If I offered you a straight-up exchange of your twenty-dollar bill for my twenty-dollar bill, would you bother to walk over and make the trade? Probably not. What's the point? If I offered you a hundred dollars to exchange with your twenty dollars, would it be worth it then? You'd make an easy eighty-dollar profit. Suddenly, there's some value for you to stand up and walk across the room.

The key, then, is to *offer more in perceived value to your patients than you are asking for in price.*

In clinical terms, if you charge seventy-five dollars for a patient visit, then your patients need to feel they're getting *more* than seventy-five dollars in value, if you want a line of patients booking to see you. If they feel like they're *just* getting seventy-five dollars in value, then it's like exchanging a twenty for a twenty—why bother leaving the house? However, if a cycle of in vitro fertilization (IVF) costs $15,000–$25,000 with a 40 percent success rate, yet twelve acupuncture sessions can double the odds of live birthrates,[1] then it is likely they will see the value in adding at least twelve acupuncture sessions to their IVF.

---

1. Hullender Rubin et al., "Impact of whole systems traditional Chinese medicine on in-vitro fertilization outcomes," *Reproductive biomedicine online* 30, no. 6 (2015): 602–12.

Is your practice set up like a commodity so that you are basically offering the same as every other acupuncturist in your area? If so, then you will need to compete for patients by being competitively priced. Over time this leads to you working harder and making less as you reduce your fees or provide free add-ons to compete and attract patients, which is the opposite of the entrepreneur's way of working less and making more.

If, on the other hand, you look for ways to provide more value, then you can absolutely charge more, and patients will be happy to pay it because they know it's worth it. And if you look, these kinds of opportunities are everywhere.

Some things we do at Acubalance to create value: Firstly, we have established ourselves as an authority in treating infertility, which is valued by both patients and referring reproductive endocrinologists (IVF clinics). We also do lots of little things that are very effective and appreciated by our patients. We provide handouts and articles for patients to read at home, as well as books they can borrow from our lending library. We spend time in the visit educating clients on what they can do at home (natural homework) to improve the effectiveness of treatments and accelerate results. We write out what we discussed at treatments and summarize it an e-mail or on paper so that they do not have to worry about remembering it. And we offer an integrative approach by discussing their case with our team of healers (TCM, ND, MD, and often other caregivers), which patients now seek out.

⊰⊱ PUT IT INTO PRACTICE ⊰⊱

Brainstorm a list of ways that you can offer services or products that would be valuable to your patients. Then put at least one of those into practice. Remember I said being successful is simple but not easy. Creating value is a continuous effort. It can take time to innovate and implement your ideas. The point is to focus on creating and providing value for your patients that will have them choose you for their care.

Part II
Success Is Surprisingly Counterintuitive

8
Whatever You've Been Thinking, Think the Opposite

The man who does more than he is paid for will soon be paid for more than he does.
—Napolean Hill

Being successful often means exploring new frontiers and going to a place where no other entrepreneur has gone before. History is filled with pioneers who were once thought crazy. And crazy they might have been, because their ideas escaped the rational mind. My point is: success is often counterintuitive.

To some extent, you've already done the opposite of what's normal if you practice complementary and alternative medicine (CAM). Most people are taught while growing up to get a regular safe, steady job. Being in business for yourself is risky and does not guarantee steady work. Most people are steered toward jobs that offer prestige or the chance for riches and early retirement such as law, accounting, or mainstream medicine. Acupuncture is not the fast track to any of those. Ever been told you're not a "real" doctor? Or that acupuncture just doesn't work? You're not alone.

So the fact that you've chosen a career in CAM is already evidence you're capable of taking the road less traveled. But the more you want to succeed at your dream, the more you're going to have to commit to letting go of doubt and the rational side of your brain.

When I first had the idea for online continuing education for functional and Chinese medicine, you would not believe how many people thought this was a bad idea. They said no one would be willing to sit through a two-hour lecture—let alone a weekend—staring into her computer from her living room. "If they see value in the lecture, regardless of being online, sure they will," I thought, especially with the added benefit of the time and money saved from not having to travel. But many of my colleagues thought I was crazy.

Obviously, this was not the case. Today, online TCM courses are the norm. The point is that the obvious is often hidden from the masses until it is revealed as a proven concept and transforms from the obscure to being obvious.

Here's another success example that came from thinking outside the box: In 2004 I suggested to the doctors in my practice that we open on Sunday, and they almost revolted. They strongly disagreed and suggested Saturday was the best weekend day to open and not Sunday. Why? They liked their Sundays, and insisted "Nobody is open on Sundays." And I—thinking from a patient-centered perspective rather than a doctor-centered one—told them that's exactly why I wanted to do it.

Saturday is still a difficult day to make it to acupuncture, because lots of people still work on Saturdays. Businesses are open, sometimes all day. It's the busiest day of the week for restaurants and retail. In Canada, the United States, and other parts of the world, even banks are open on Saturdays. It's a real shopping day.

But Sunday, people want to relax, which acupuncture is great for. For the professionals and working individuals who comprise our primary clientele base, it's far and away the best day for them. Traffic's easier. Parking's easier. They aren't rushing from work or trying to cram an acupuncture appointment into an already full schedule of errands.

So I told our doctors, "Let's experiment with it. I think it'll work, but I'm not attached to it, so let's give it three months and if we don't like it, we'll go back to being closed on Sundays and revisit Saturday."

It took one month for our Sunday schedule to become full and it's been our busiest clinic day ever since. We're booked out on Sundays months in advance. And it's wonderful. The patients love it, because they aren't rushing from work and trying to cram an appointment into their lunch hour. And we love it, too. The phones don't ring as much, which makes it easier on our admin staff. And the practitioners love having a day that's always full and rarely has last-minute cancellations, which makes it more profitable for them. When one of our doctors went on maternity leave, the doctor who came in to cover her at first didn't want to treat on Sundays, but after she got a taste of it, she didn't want to give it back.

So whatever you think, think the opposite. You just might find that it was your best idea yet.

⊰❧ PUT IT INTO PRACTICE ❧⊱

Ignore the Naysayers

If you are going to be a pioneer, an entrepreneur, and a leader in your field, then you have to be able to block out all the negative noise and the background chatter. That stuff will always be there. But the naysayers do not have your vision. You have the vision of the right life for you, and only you can fulfill it.

Interrupt the Emotion-Logic Paradigm

Contrary to popular belief, humans are not rational beings. We are emotional beings who often use logic to make sense of our emotions. So next time you have an idea for your practice, especially if no one else is doing it or it seems counterintuitive, if your immediate thought is, "That won't work because . . ." recognize that this is just your brain trying to apply logic to some emotional reaction.

When that happens, take a second to think about it a

little more. Meditate on it or write in a journal—whatever gets your mental juices flowing. Look into the future. Envision how it might work. And if you think you can make it work, do it!

9
Nice Guys Finish Last

Nice guys finish last.
—A FAMOUS SPORTS QUOTE

The idea that ruthlessness is the way to succeed in business is promoted by everyone from Machiavelli to Donald Trump. But this idea is no more accurate than the notion that money is evil. You don't have to be coldhearted to be successful. In fact, many successful people are kind and generous. They're just not pushovers.

Now, let's be realistic. Human psychology makes it almost impossible to ignore what others think of us. We all want to be liked, right? Do you know anyone who goes out of his way to upset others and collect enemies? Probably not.

And yet, many of the people we most admire upset a lot of people on their way to success. Think about Nelson Mandela, Mahatma Gandhi, or Martin Luther King Jr. Think about Abraham Lincoln, who brought the United States into a war in order to keep it together. All of these people created enemies, were ridiculed, and faced extraordinary challenges in the court of public opinion. So how do you find the balance to achieve success in an industry whose very business is balance?

As with everything, it starts with attitude. For successful people like the ones mentioned above, popularity was not their primary concern. Now, I am not advocating intentionally hurting others to get what you want. What I am suggesting is that when you challenge others' belief systems and ways of doing things, you will almost always attract resistance. As I said in the last chapter, part of innovation is to overcome the objections of others.

There's been a recent movement toward community acupuncture—acupuncture performed in a group setting, with many patients receiving treatment at once, as it's traditionally done in Asia, as opposed to the Western one-on-one model.

The advantages should be obvious. It allows the practitioner to treat more people per hour, maintaining the same (or greater) revenue for the practitioner while offering a more affordable option to less-affluent patients. But the opposition to this new way of doing things has been considerable. Some have argued that the one-on-one setup is critical to effective treatment and that a practitioner can't give a complete, personalized diagnosis in a group setting. Others have argued it's a violation of patient privacy.

If the founders of this model were concerned about being liked by their colleagues, then they would have never been able to stand up for what they felt is the right thing for them and their patients. But this doesn't mean the pioneers of community acupuncture are mean, amoral, or self-centered people. Chances are they are nice. (Matthew Bauer, founder of the Acupuncture Now Foundation, who reviewed my book, shared this about the founders of community acupuncture: "They are more than nice people—they are about as compassionate and caring as any people you will ever meet."

But these individuals had to stick with their beliefs and goals despite that opposition. Sometimes, going against the grain means getting a few splinters. If you want to be successful, you have to be willing to do that.

After all, which is truly the "nicer" course of action: doing something different that may not be immediately received well by the masses but ultimately benefits your practice and your patients, or running yourself ragged, trying to be well liked? Strive to do good, rather than be nice. Success will follow. If you are doing something that is great but different, then it is inevitable you will pick up a few enemies along the way. But you will also pick up raving fans, too.

◈ PUT IT INTO PRACTICE ◈

Ask yourself: What aren't you doing because you're afraid of what others will think of you? Where are you being nice at the expense of following your dream? Be courageous and follow your truth to help benefit others, even it means rocking the boat.

10
Free Has No Value

*I had to live in the desert
before I could understand the full
value of grass in a green ditch.*
—Ella Maillart

You can't go anywhere these days without getting bombarded by free stuff. Grocery store coupons, Internet downloads, apps, e-books, promotional giveaways, door prizes, product samples, pens with company logos, furniture left on the side of the road, and the list is practically endless. There are whole websites devoted to things that are free (www.freestuff.com). There's a free section on Craigslist. You can take a free class or download a free e-book on just about anything.

But free, as it turns out, has no value.

Think about it: At the end of a meal, which are you more likely to leave unfinished: a full glass of water, or a full glass of wine? How many free e-books have you downloaded that you barely even looked at? When you were in college or acupuncture school, who were the better students—the kids whose parents were paying for everything, or the ones who were paying for all of it themselves?

Canada's Work and Compensation Board has discovered that people receiving workers' compensation take longer to recover from injuries than people who have to get back to work in order to pay their bills.

It's really a simple equation. When you've invested in something, you care about it. You want to see it turn out well. You want to ensure that you've extracted all the value you can from it. But when it's free, there's no pressure to extract that value, so you no longer care about it as much.

As a practitioner, giving free or discounted services on a regular basis can very quickly turn you into an acupuncture thrift store. Have you given free initial consults, or used Groupon to attract new patients, or discounted services to someone who said right off the bat that they couldn't afford you? Have you found that those patients tend to cancel, no-show, or show up late at higher rates than your full-paying patients? That's certainly been my experience, and it's been the experience of other practitioners I have interviewed, too.

Patients who don't pay invariably take their treatments less seriously than those who pay. If they really wanted what you had to offer, they'd figure out a way to afford you. The fact that they're unwilling to pay the full fee for your service is usually evidence not that they need help financially, but rather that they don't value your product or service as much as you are charging.

But it gets worse. The demographic of patients you treat

are the ones you also continue to attract, as they will refer their friends who will want the same discounts. No one wants to pay more than their friend is paying. So if you regularly offer discount pricing, the patients you attract will be deal seekers—who are not only less passionate about whatever they're buying, but *they're going to refer other deal seekers.* Before you know it, you could wind up with a practice full of people looking for—even demanding—rock-bottom prices.

How about patients whose insurance covers some or all of their treatment? Many acupuncturists think insurance is the Holy Grail; that it would save their practices if insurance covered acupuncture. Unfortunately, I've had patients stop halfway through a treatment plan—even though things were going extremely well—when they suddenly found out their work insurance only covered a certain amount of acupuncture.

This may sound counterintuitive, but I've had the following happen to me, and have interviewed other practitioners who've had the same experience. My patient has experienced great relief, and she's about 75 percent better. She's spent, say, $600 on six treatments and I offer to continue to treat her for a few more weeks with the hopes of providing her with 100 percent relief, at a cost of $300 in treatments. So she's spent $600 so far, is very happy with her progress and is prepared to spend another $300 for a total of $900 for even more relief.

Then she finds out she has extended medical insurance covered through work that allows $500 annually in acupuncture. *And she cancels her remaining visits.*

Logic dictates she would have been happy to continue with treatments, because she was prepared to invest $900 before she learned she had some coverage, and now it will only cost her $400 out of pocket. But she didn't continue. Why?

I think the coverage creates a sense of entitlement. In her mind, rather than feeling she just saved $500 toward a $900 investment, she feels she spent $100 too much for her allotted free acupuncture for the year. The $500 of free acupuncture basically diminishes the value.

Remember, this is not a hypothetical situation—this is a scenario we have witnessed many times. Patients are programmed to come in only for what insurance will cover. When treatment is free, they don't want to spend anything. They'll come back next year when the insurance comes back. Insurance just devalued your service and also created a sense of entitlement.

Now, sometimes I do discount my services. I just recognize that when I do so, it is a form of charity. I have set a budget for how many sessions I'm willing to discount or give away for the year, I stick to that plan, and I can afford to do so because the rest of my patients are on standard pricing.

To put it into perspective, working people do not give all their earnings away to charity. They budget a certain amount for charity, or tithing, to support their community. And I do recommend you give to charity, because you're part of a community that needs and deserves your support.

However, I never advertise discounts, and if a new patient comes in asking for one, I'll always say no. The people we offer discounts to are the ones who have been coming regularly, are clearly committed to their treatment, but we can tell one way or another that they're struggling financially. Those people are very grateful for the support, and for being offered the discount without having to ask.

Usually, the way I do this is by giving free treatments at the end of a series. If they're coming in for ten visits and I'm planning on discounting it 30 percent, instead of knocking 30 percent off every visit, I'll charge full price for the first seven and the last three for free. This way they're more likely to come in for those last few treatments, and they will get better results by completing the series of ten treatments.

Whatever you do, the point is to make sure that the patients have something at stake, that they're invested in their treatment. The second you devalue yourself is the second you start struggling to get people to pay you what you really want. Ask for what you're worth, and budget how much charity work you want to offer.

✥ PUT IT INTO PRACTICE ✥

Decide how much you're going to give away this year and how you're going to do it. Figure out how many treatments that is per week, month, or year. If a patient needs a price break, then structure it in a way that they need to complete the majority of your treatment plan before they receive the discount or freebie. This prevents you from devaluing your services and motivates them to complete your program so that they actually receive the benefit from your treatments.

11
Big Fish in a Small Pond

*Be faithful to that which exists
nowhere but in yourself—and thus
make yourself indispensable.*
—André Gide

Some people feel that specialization goes counter to the holistic nature of Chinese medicine, because we're supposed to focus on treating the person and not the disease. But to think specialization focuses only on the condition without looking at the individual as a whole is nothing more than a myth.

Back in 2002, when I decided to specialize in infertility, my colleagues thought I was crazy. Practitioners at the time would see maybe two to four infertility patients per year. My colleagues told me I would starve because there was not the patient population to support a practice dedicated to treating infertility—a condition that doesn't even get its own disease category (like menstrual pain or heavy bleeding) in Chinese gynecology textbooks, but rather falls under "miscellaneous diseases."

The first problem, of course, is that all my colleagues were thinking from their perspective and not the patients'. When you have a heart attack, do you want to see a general practitioner, or do you want to see a cardiologist? Personally, I would seek out the heart specialist who has had additional training in treating heart patients and who has seen hundreds or thousands of heart cases.

If you have a fear of heights and had your choice of therapists, would you choose one that lists twenty fears and phobias, of which heights is one, or would you prefer a therapist who specializes only in the treatment of fear of heights? All other factors being equal, you'd probably choose the therapist who specializes in your condition over the generalist. You'd probably even pay more for that one, because you would assume you'll have a greater chance of success if all she treats is fear of heights.

Achieving mastery provides you with the benefit of becoming a big fish in a small pond. When you choose to focus on a specific patient group, you quickly become the authority in that area. You separate yourself from the pack. You become easy to refer to. Word gets around that you are the person to see, and even other TCM practitioners will refer you some of their patients that you specialize in treating. Patients will begin to seek you out and they will travel to see you even if a general practitioner is located closer. Many are willing to pay more for a specialist because they see the value in seeing an expert.

Note, you can't just say you're specializing in this one area and just leave it at that. You actually have to put the work in. You need to study and learn everything you can about it so that you actually become the expert.

And for the record, specializing in a particular condition doesn't make TCM any less holistic. When a patient visits about infertility, I still do a full intake, which includes a detailed history taking, observation, pulse, and tongue. I formulate a TCM pattern differential diagnosis based on my initial intake. I ask her for any and all symptoms— headaches, night sweats, hot flashes, irregular periods, constipation, et cetera—and I look at them holistically. Infertility is the disease; in applying TCM principles, I uncover the underlying cause(s) and address the pattern leading to her infertility.

Today, my clinic offers more than forty fertility treatments per day. This is another example of ignoring the naysayers, and how being a big fish in a small pond can build you a very busy and rewarding practice.

Hopefully, you see how your specialization can actually be *more* holistic and *more* patient centered, allowing you the ability to give the best possible care of your patients. Remember, you still need to treat patients as individuals and not just address their disease. Your specialty helps you attract a certain demographic to your practice, being the ailment in which you specialize.

❧ PUT IT INTO PRACTICE ❧

No one's going to force you to specialize if you don't want to, but it's worth exploring the state of your local market.

First, make a list of areas within TCM you might be interested in specializing in. These may be conditions you've already seen quite a bit, or maybe they're just topics you're interested in. You can also look for demographics where people are motivated to find a solution. I predict the following specialties will be growth markets in the coming years:

- Infertility
- Pregnancy support—This is a special time in a woman's life, and women are looking for non-drug approaches for relief from morning sickness, back pain, breech presentations, and to assist in a positive birth experience.
- Dermatology—Itching, inflamed, or problematic skin conditions will motivate people to seek you out.
- Pediatrics—Parents don't want to see their child suffer, and Chinese medicine is a safe and natural approach to treating kids and keeping them well.
- Insomnia—This is a condition more people are dealing with than ever before.

I also recommend watching the one-hour medigogy webinar by ABORM president Chris Axelrad, *The Benefits of Specialization in Acupuncture and Chinese Medicine*, found in the recording archives on Medigogy.com.

Remember, no matter what you specialize in, you're still treating the underlying cause and addressing the pattern imbalance and not just the disease.

12
Delegate

Only do what only you can do.
—Paul Sloane

Small-business owners eventually reach a ceiling where they would be better off hiring support staff than continuing to do everything themselves. This ceiling is the peak of earnings and the peak of what we can accomplish on our own. In this environment, substantial growth seems to stagnate. But we are usually resistant to giving up tasks to others to allow pushing through this ceiling.

I can't speak for others as to why this is the case, but I can say from my personal experience that it was partly because I feared it would not be done the way I wanted it to be done (yes, entrepreneurs have some control issues) and partly because I was too busy to hire and train properly.

Here is a secret that I shared when I was interviewed for a business magazine: You need to hire *in advance* of your needs. Waiting until you reach your ceiling can cause major problems.

Financially this is more challenging, but it pays off by allowing you time to make sure you're hiring the right people, and by allowing you to grow into your capacity, rather than struggling to overcome it.

I like to use the fishbowl analogy. A fish grows based on the size of the container it's placed in: a small bowl yields a small fish; a large tank yields a large fish. But if the fish grows to adulthood in a small bowl and then you try to transfer it, it won't grow any larger. For it to be bigger, it needs to have been in the larger tank from infancy.

Likewise, managing all the day-to-day activities of running your business leaves you no room to grow. If all your time is spent on things that *have* to be done—like bookkeeping, taxes, answering phones, or vacuuming—you do not have sufficient time left for treating, speaking engagements, developing relationships with potential referral sources, writing articles, or learning more about your field. These are all necessary parts of growing your practice (we'll talk more about them in part III), and they're things that only you can do. Those other things, anyone can do. Without delegating those other tasks, your practice can't expand.

The other issue is one of quality. Delegation is not simply about giving away tasks you dislike, but giving you the time to focus on what you do best. If you are doing the accounting but are not a good accountant, it might consume hours of your day on a weekly basis, you might make mistakes, or you might get frustrated, which then diminishes your ability to provide a calm and nurturing environment to your patients. Hiring an expert to do those things takes all those challenges away from you, leaving you free to actually treat people.

Furthermore, if you wait to hire until you are busy, you're more likely to make hiring mistakes because you lack the time to search for the best possible candidate. You won't be able to properly train that person. You'll end up spending a ton of time trying to support him while he gets up to speed—time which, as busy as you are, you cannot afford.

All of these factors conspire to take away from the quality you provide as a practitioner, which means that all the great service that made you busy is all for naught. Your clients become less happy. Your business may shrink, or you may lose personal job satisfaction. None of these are good scenarios.

Only Do What Only You Can Do

Support staff can be a significant expense for some. But remember our discussion from chapter 4 about cost versus ROI.

I have a bookkeeper for my practice—even though, if you remember, I worked as a chartered professional accountant (CPA) for a decade and I am equally qualified and skilled to do my clinic accounting and taxes as those offering bookkeeping services. Nevertheless, this is a task I've delegated because on the days I treat patients, I see three per hour, and on the days I don't I give public talks, write articles, create continuing education courses, and otherwise work on growing my business. If I didn't have a bookkeeper, I'd have to take time off from one of those tasks, which would either reduce my billable hours (by much more than the forty dollars per hour I'm paying her) or reduce the growth of my business. So I hire somebody to do my books even though I am qualified to do them myself because I can generate more income per hour than my bookkeeper's cost.

All of which is to say: focus not on the cost, but on the ROI. You can also use support techs for certain activities. Your doctor does not take your X-rays, do your ultrasound, or draw your blood. They have nurses and technicians who do that. Likewise, you can have acupuncture assistants who do moxibustion, prep your patients, and so forth. Each jurisdiction has its own scope of practice and legalities regarding assistants. Please check with your specific regulatory body and jurisdictions if it is legal and within your scope to have an assistant.

Last but not least, the front office is the place every practice should be delegating and delegating *right*. The job of your front office is to keep your patients smiling throughout their TCM experience, and a good receptionist can add tremendous value. We actually had one receptionist who was so good, when she went on maternity leave our business went down—she was so excellent at answering questions and giving patients the confidence that we were the right choice, they always booked when speaking with her. Make sure that the person you hire believes in what you offer, is an excellent communicator, has a great bedside manner, and comes with zero entitlement. Also, hire someone who wants to work in this field—maybe who wants to be an office manager, or is training to be a TCM practitioner—not someone who just needs something to pay the bills while they find the job they really want (e.g., as a teacher or counselor). I've learned this the hard way, hiring great people who left after several months when they found jobs in their field. They all departed on very good terms, but nevertheless we were left with gaps in our front office that on one occasion almost paralyzed us.

Finally, remember that there's more to delegation than hiring staff. You can put systems into place, too: online booking, scheduling packages, virtual assistants, et cetera. They each have their own pros and cons. While I prefer the in-person help, these other systems are definitely valid. And of course, combinations of systems and in-person help can be used to great effect. Evaluating how these different options can benefit you and your practice is a key step in expansion.

Whatever you choose, the people you bring into your practice should have the same passion, drive, and commitment to excellence that you hold yourself to. Hire them and delegate to them now to keep things from getting out of hand.

⊰⊱ PUT IT INTO PRACTICE ⊰⊱

Take some time to go through your practice and see (1) what you aren't doing that you'd like to be doing to grow your practice, and (2) where it might best behoove you to hire support staff or utilize a service to give you more time.

Part III
Growing Your Practice

13
Associates

*Train people well enough so they
can leave; treat them well enough
so they don't want to.*

—Sir Richard Branson

Once your practice has more patients than you can treat
yourself (a lengthy waiting list), you'll have to choose
between raising your fees, working more hours, turning
patients away, or hiring associates to treat the overflow.
It's a good problem to have, but it's an important one to
manage correctly.

Associates are great because they allow you to generate
extra income and shorten your waiting list, allowing you
to keep patients in your practice who otherwise might go
elsewhere. The only downside, if there is one, is that you'll
probably see a temporary dip in profit while the new doctor
fills her schedule. Basically it's three steps backward, ten
steps forward. But in my experience, recovering from that
dip happens fairly quickly, and soon my associate becomes
busier and my schedule returns to capacity.

Basically, you're just making the pie a lot bigger, so

someone else can enjoy a good living and you increase your income in the process. As long as you create value for your associates (by sending them referrals, offering a supportive environment in which to practice and master their skills, and giving them room for growth and some autonomy), they will continue to work toward the vision of the practice, and before long you will be making more than you were making before you hired them. Eventually, you can have enough associates practicing under your clinic umbrella to afford you the time to take on other projects and to perhaps treat less, if that is your desire.

You could also add other modalities that complement your patient population: for example, a massage therapist, chiropractor, naturopathic physician, or medical doctor. These are great services that can cover overhead, and they'll bring in new patients who can cross over to other services.

Doctors and Managers

Unfortunately, hiring associates is not truly passive income where you can sit back and play all day. You can't just put your associates into the bank and live off the interest. Even though they will generate revenue for you, they still require your time to manage and supervise if you are the clinic owner. They're human beings. You need to hire them, listen to their needs, teach them your systems, give them encouragement and constructive criticism, help them grow, and so on. Basically, you are the conductor of the orchestra. If you hire for culture fit and avoid those infected with entitlement syndrome, then it can be a very positive and fruitful venture for all involved. I failed miserably in my early years at being a leader for my associates. I thought feeding them patients was enough. By assembling a non-cohesive team, it required a lot of my time managing the clinic and dealing with office drama. There were periods of time where it was not enjoyable for many of us to come to work. I eventually took responsibility for all the issues and invested in myself to develop my leadership skills. It has only been in the past few years that we have assembled an incredible team at Acubalance. We all work hard, but we have lots of fun and we are all prospering, too. The beauty of having a good team and the same players for many years who are self-motivated, dedicated to supporting their team members, flexible, and hardworking (some of the qualities we look for when hiring at Acubalance) is they need very little managing from me.

So now you need to ask yourself a question: Do you want to manage a clinic or be a doctor? People need to be managed, and they need somebody responsible for the clinic to make sure you're all part of the same vision and the same dream—if one of them gets out of tune, it can throw off the whole orchestra. So as your practice grows, you'll need to choose. Once you have several associates and find that you're spending most of your time managing and marketing, if that's what you love to do, great! But if you would rather be seeing patients, hire an office manager to do those things for you. I promise, if you are not skilled at the managerial responsibilities for running a clinic, you'll be much happier if you delegate those duties to someone else.

⋙ PUT IT INTO PRACTICE ⋙

If your waiting list is longer than two weeks, consider raising your fees or hiring an associate! And whether you have a list or not, ask yourself whether your patients would benefit from some of the additional services suggested above, and see about bringing in one of those specialists. And it is worth repeating: avoid hiring anyone who has entitlement syndrome.

14
Choose Your Ideal Client

Everyone is not your customer.
—SETH GODIN

Do you ever look at your schedule and see a name that makes your stomach sink? A chronic complainer, a nonbeliever, or maybe someone who always shows up late and throws your schedule off? Does that person have a tendency to ruin your whole day? Sap the energy from you and your staff, creating an unhealthy atmosphere that seeps into your interactions with other clients?

Do you want to build your entire practice full of this kind of difficult client? Of course not.

According to the 80/20 rule (otherwise known as the Pareto principle or "the law of the vital few"), 80 percent of your time is consumed by 20 percent of your customers. That is, you'll spend most of your energy—emotional, physical, or otherwise—dealing with the people who comprise just a small percentage of your patient base.

This has some pretty stunning implications when you

think about it. In particular it means that surprising as it may sound, *you don't need to treat everyone who walks through your front door.*

The patients coming to see you should respect your abilities, trust your methods, and be eager to invest in their own well-being through the treatment process. They should value your time and expertise. And if they don't, you should convert them to your ideal patient if you can, or if you can't, then help them find another practitioner as soon as possible. Remember, it all starts with attitude, so as counterintuitive as it may seem to turn away a paying customer—and as uncomfortable as it may be to have the conversation—I promise that continuing to treat them indefinitely is far, far worse.

The following are red-flag behaviors in patients I watch out for:

- finding fault and cannot be satisfied;
- verbally abusing me or my staff;
- arguing about fees or constantly asking for discounts;
- constantly canceling, rescheduling, or no-showing; or
- not complying with my treatment recommendations and blaming me for their lack of progress.

If you have clients showing behaviors like these, let them know what you expect of them, or that this relationship isn't going to work. In the spirit of Chinese medicine, make sure you show compassion and empathy—and to quote Dr. Leon Hammer, *"they did not come to you to be difficult, they came to you to heal and not be difficult anymore."* They just don't know how to do that, and maybe you can't seem to help them. At the same time, remember it's not in your power to satisfy everybody and if you keep trying, you will waste your valuable time on them, instead of on the people you can really make a difference with.

You also need to have an official (written) cancellation policy in place. I require all of my patients to sign this policy as part of their new-patient paperwork, stating that they understand that any last-minute cancellations or no-shows are still charged the full amount. (What constitutes last minute is up to you, but 24–48 hours is fairly standard.) A policy like this demonstrates that you value your own time, and the patient should also. Now, of course you can be lenient for special circumstances. If a client is usually on time but has a family emergency or is sick, then it's perfectly reasonable to waive the charge. The cancellation policy is about setting boundaries and expectations as well as communicating that you value your time and they need to as well.

Practitioners who are just starting out or are otherwise struggling to fill their practice might be a bit hesitant to enforce the cancellation policy or to kindly "fire" patients if they are not the right fit. At the beginning, everybody thinks they have to take every patient on, and they're worried about paying the bills. But trust me, this all goes back to attitude. Being able to stay focused on your dream practice and maintain an entrepreneurial attitude is crucial to your success in practice. And remember that the clients you accept as patients will likely refer their friends and families who could be similar to them as well.

◄◈► PUT IT INTO PRACTICE ◄◈►

Let Go of the 20 Percent

Take some time to go through your current client list. Have your associates and office staff do the same. Highlight the names of anyone who fits one of the problem categories above, and then commit to having a conversation with them about how you expect people to treat your staff, or your expectations of them and their active role (diet, lifestyle, treatment schedule) if they want to get the results. Start with the easy ones, and then move on to the harder cases once you see how much of an impact the positive shift has had on your practice. What is not an option is that they remain difficult and consume your time and energy.

Remember there is nothing to fear as your difficult clients are both time and energy zappers. You must have good *wei qi* (defense qi) to protect your *jing* (vital essence). If your difficult patient chooses not to rebook because of the conversation you had with them or the healthy boundaries you establish, then this frees up time for an ideal client to book in. Basically, you want them to either become ideal clients or choose not to return. Being difficult is not an option. You will have much better job satisfaction if you fill your practice with your ideal clients.

Recruit More Ideal Clients

Make a list of your "favorite" clients you treat—the ones you enjoy seeing on your schedule. What qualities do they have in common? Where can you find more of them? How can you recruit them into your practice? Identify them, create a plan for recruiting similar patients, and then put it into action.

15

Bridges and Stepping-Stones

*In marketing I've seen only one strategy that
can't miss—and that is to market to your
best customers first, your best prospects
second, and the rest of the world last.*
—John Romero

The sole purpose of marketing is to create *mind share*: to
tell the people who don't know about you that you exist,
and to remind the people who do know about you that
you're still here.

Business coach and entrepreneur Dan Clements has a
great metaphor for marketing in his book *The Practitioner's
Journey: The Path to Success for Alternative, Holistic &
Integrative Health Professionals*: On one side of a big
riverbank are all the patients who could use your service,
and on the other side of this river is you. You want them
to come see you, but they don't know you're there. So
you need to make them aware. You can shout across the
river (i.e., put up a website or an ad), and now they see

you, but if the water's too cold or too deep, or it's moving a little too rapidly, or they're just lazy, they aren't going to come across.

To help them past those risks and obstacles, Clements introduces the idea of using *stepping-stones* and *bridges*. Stepping-stones you place in the water to encourage someone to move a little bit closer. Usually the stones won't get that someone all the way across the river, but they're a step in the right direction. And the more stepping-stones you lay down, the more likely they are to get all the way across. Stepping-stones, then, are about persistently getting your name out there and making yourself an attractive medical choice.

Bridges, on the other hand, will get patients to you directly. Some of them may be harder to build, but they circumvent all the other obstacles, so potential clients can cross right over to where you are. In practice terms, bridges are solid referral relationships.

There are hundreds of great books out there that discuss marketing, so I'm not going to go into too much depth here. But as a TCM practitioner, the following stepping-stones and bridges work well for my practice.

Stepping-Stones

Fifteen-minute complimentary consults—I'm not talking about a free treatment. This is an introduction, like the preview to a movie. The purpose is for them to determine if you can help them and if they feel comfortable being in your care. We regularly have people who come in for a free fifteen-minute consult that turns into a paid visit by the end—after ten minutes they communicate they feel comfortable and confident that they have found the right clinic and ask to have their initial session right there and then.

Acupuncture happy hour—Once a month I go to a local fertility clinic for an hour or two to give the medical staff (nurses, doctors, and embryologist) and admin staff twenty minutes of stress-reduction acupuncture treatments. I use a standard protocol of ear and scalp points and some body points (max. six needles), but just some basic acupuncture to create a relaxation response. This is something that the fertility clinic gets to offer as a free value added to their staff. Acupuncture happy hour is a great way to introduce and allow new and past clients to experience the benefits of acupuncture. I suggest you follow up with each person after the happy hour to see if they are interested in setting up a full consult and treatment. Some TCM practitioners will do these at their practices, too, as a way for patients to refer their friends. However you do it, just make sure to use a consent form that includes their contact information so you can reach out to them afterward.

Ads and listings—Newspapers, websites, Acufinder, and so on. Remember that stepping-stones are about persistence; that goes double here. The reason you see the same commercials on TV over and over again is not because the advertisers think you haven't seen it, it's because they know the average person needs to see something six times before they'll take action. Think about that—if you spend money on a single ad, you're just throwing your money away. If you repeat the ad numerous times so that the average customer sees your ad five times or more, then you'll start to see gains.

So, yes, you should have a website. Yes, you should be listed on sites so that your clients can find you. But once you start talking about ads and spending money, you really need a long-term comprehensive plan to make it work effectively.

The other important note here is to make sure there's a call to action on every advertisement: "Come in for a free initial consult," "register for a free talk," "download a copy of XYZ," et cetera. Without the call to action, you're creating awareness but not helping them get across the river. If the ad is one stepping-stone, the call to action is a second. And remember, you need as many of them as possible to get people to you.

Writing—Articles in magazines, weekly blog posts, or e-newsletters are a huge opportunity to establish yourself as an authority. Getting one published in a trade or customer-facing publication is a great way to build your credibility, but you don't need to be in the *New York Times* for the article to make a difference. Posting articles anywhere creates value and engages your current and potential clients. (Don't forget your call to action!) The first people to market to are your current clients. Help build your patients' confidence in you and maintain mind share by sending a newsletter out to them in October, reminding them to use up their acupuncture insurance before year end, discussing a new acupuncture study that came out, letting them know about a new workshop you attended to treat XYX, sharing a success story, et cetera.

If you are considered an authority in a particular area, you can use press releases to let people know about a new service, new research, or how to treat a particular condition. I generally send at least three press releases per year. The key is to make them timely and relevant: infertility awareness weeks, mental health days, acupuncture awareness week, heart health months, when there is big news about a particular disease, and so forth.

And if you're feeling really ambitious, write a book. This is your big business card, and one of the best stepping-stones because it's a massive one that can have a domino effect—it makes you an authority, can land you some media attention, helps you get public speaking events, and can really build your practice. Naturally, it's also one of the hardest to achieve—it takes a lot of effort to write a book, and then you have to market it as well as your practice. (Of course the two are intertwined.)

Networking—There are formal, highly organized groups such as BNI International; smaller, informal local mixers and events; and a thousand others in between. Networking events help to create awareness and connections with others in your field, and often lead to referrals and other great working relationships. And some of these relationships can turn into bridges.

Public talks—These can be small info sessions at your clinic or at independent locations (Whole Foods, a regional clinic, community center, etc.), or they can be large events at conferences. Either way, if you have good communication and presentation skills, they can be very powerful. (And if you don't have those skills, develop them!) Public talks marry the best features of writing and networking—they give you the opportunity to establish yourself as an expert in the community, and they also build trust and relationships.

Reactivation—Remember, the best way to build your practice is to market to your best customers first. Call or e-mail patients you have not seen in a while and check in to see how they are doing. Of course, when a patient just pops into your mind, you could call them then, but you can also take a more organized approach. Set a process to call patients three months after their last visit. Send patients birthday or Christmas cards. I send out an e-mail at the first of every month, inviting those having birthdays this month to come in during the week of their birthday to receive a discount off their treatment. They get a percentage off that amounts to their age—29 percent off if you're turning twenty-nine, 76 percent if you're turning seventy-six, and so forth.

Testimonials—Testimonials can be put on your website and blog, used in ads and press releases, and can help boost press for your books and public talks. Testimonials also help in reactivating old patients and enrolling new patients. Patients have shared with me that they came in to my clinic because they read a testimonial on the Acubalance.ca website that resonated with them and gave them confidence and hope that their specific concern was treatable.

Ask for referrals—Word of mouth is one of the most powerful marketing methods because it relies entirely on whether current or past clients like what you did for them. When a patient of mine is acting particularly grateful, I'll tell them, "I really enjoy treating patients like you (with their condition, certain personality trait, etc.). If you know anyone else who might want to see me, please send them my way." You'd be amazed at the kind of reasons people come up with for not having referred their friends (e.g., "You always seem so busy; I didn't know if you had time to see them"). Just putting it out there like that gets people thinking about referring you. It's the call to action, in verbal form.

Thank-you notes, e-mails, and newsletters with sharable tools and resources are also good places in which to ask for referrals.

SEO and SEM—To the uninitiated, these stand for search engine optimization and search engine marketing. The former means setting up your website so that when people search for an acupuncturist in your area, you're the one who shows up organically in the search results. The latter refers to paid ads so that when they perform that same search, you show up as a sponsored link.

It's really important to learn about these tools, because *just setting up a website is not enough.* If you build your site without optimizing it, the only people who will find it are the ones who already know about you (i.e., saw an ad, your business card, etc.). If you want your website to help generate leads for new patients, SEO and SEM are the tools to make it happen.

These are both huge topics, and there are hundreds, possibly thousands of companies out there that do nothing but this. I recommend you hire one of those companies. They're usually not cheap, but remember the ROI. If you spend $300 a month on SEM, how many new patients do you need to bring in, and for how many visits each, for your campaign to be profitable?

Bridges

Professional referrals—When doctors tell their patients to see you for treatment, it acts as a bridge and removes most obstacles and fears from crossing the water to reach you. Patients will connect with you most of the time if they receive a strong recommendation from another health-care provider.

The way you make this happen is to build rapport with medical professionals. People do business with people they like and whose offerings they genuinely appreciate. Just like with patients, you need to create value for your referral sources, so do your research and talk to them about how you can benefit them, not just how they can benefit you.

For example: Most physicians don't believe that acupuncture can actually treat infertility. If I were to pitch to them that it does, they'd dismiss me and I'd never get anywhere. So I don't pitch to them based on that. What I tell them is that acupuncture can reduce stress and increase blood flow to the reproductive organs. And when patients are less stressed, they become less demanding of their physicians. They're more pleasant to be around; they make their doctors' lives easier.

Who wouldn't want that? Now I'm not trying to take their job away, I'm trying to make their lives easier and improve their relationships with their patients. That's a much, much easier sell. And I have research supporting the stress-reduction effects and their ability to increase blood flow as well.

Relationship building takes time—often years—so be prepared to be patient and persistent. Drug reps visit physicians monthly because they know a very fundamental truth: out of sight, out of mind. Just like with those TV ads. So when you're building those relationships, remember that this is a marathon, not a sprint. Buy them lunch, or invite them to speak alongside you at a public appearance. Create value for them (do not be a taker) and be interested in the long-term relationship. And once you have that referral relationship, once a month send an e-mail, visit the doctors, send a Chinese New Year basket, make sure they have enough stock of your pamphlets, et cetera. This will help you stay fresh in their mind without overwhelming them.

Marketing can be very expensive. Whichever methods you decide to use, remember the purpose is *mind share and laying down stepping-stones so that clients can reach your clinic doorstep.* And if the costs start to build up, remember to think of the ROI. Marketing when set up as effective stepping-stones can be a worthwhile investment. Many of the ideas above are free or cost minimally. Just remember your call to action.

⚜ PUT IT INTO PRACTICE ⚜

Look over the different marketing techniques above. Pick at least one new technique you can start to implement immediately, and take action on it! Then read the next two chapters of this book, which will help to turn this somewhat overwhelming list into a more concrete action plan.

16
Mind the Gap

We are what we repeatedly do. Excellence,
then, is not an act, but a habit.
—ARISTOTLE

Strategic coach Dan Sullivan has written *Learning How to Avoid the Gap,* which uses the following analogy: Imagine you're sailing across the ocean. Ahead in the distance you see a horizon—which is just an illusion where it appears that the sky meets the ocean. The horizon signifies our long-term goal(s). For patients, it signifies the magical end to their problems: no back pain, no headaches, normal blood pressure, an end to sleepless nights, a baby, whatever it may be. For us as TCM practitioners, it might be a full practice, or an abundance of income that affords us the luxury and comfort of freedom to do whatever we want, or the ability to take well-deserved holidays or pay for our kids' college education.

But as you're sailing across the ocean, the horizon never seems to get closer. Every morning as you return on deck from your sleeping quarters and look out at the horizon, it will appear every bit as far away as it did the day before.

If you focus only on the horizon and do not regularly check behind you to see how far you have traveled from land, then it's easy to get depressed and frustrated and to lose your confidence because it appears you are not making any progress. But that's because you are only focusing on the horizon, what you have yet to achieve.

This is the gap.

It is very important to set goals if you want to be successful, but you also need to regularly stop to measure your progress and appreciate your milestones along the way. Just like the horizon, your goals can keep eluding you as you change them or you choose bigger goals. It is human nature to constantly strive to be better. Just like the horizon, we can never truly reach our full potential, so it is important to avoid the gap by regularly looking back and acknowledging how far you have come since you started.

———

Measure Progress in Reality

Remember, the gap applies to both you and your patients. Your patients may have come in with back pain that they rated ten out of ten and were taking four painkillers per day. If they fail to notice that after a month of treatment, the pain has reduced to a three out of ten and now only one painkiller a day, they may say, "This isn't working; I still have back pain," and convince themselves that it's a lost hope. So you must remind them of the progress they have made.

Infertility can take several months to over a year to treat.

Along the way, there are all kinds of symptoms a patient presents with that can point to an underlying cause—for example, PMS, irregular cycles, painful periods, blood quality, poor digestion, stress, weight. If a patient comes in for six months and still isn't pregnant, it's likely she would just quit if I didn't make it a point of documenting, at each visit, what she is experiencing. Then, once a month or so, I do a complete reevaluation, review all her symptoms, and then show her where we have made progress and where we still have room for improvement. A patient will look at that horizon, thinking, "I want a baby," and forget that six months ago she was on six Naproxen a day for four days for her painful periods, and now she only needs one pill and only on day one. Doing that reevaluation I get to remind her of that and celebrate her progress with her, and this often motivates her to finish the course of treatment that allows me to address the underlying causes to her subfertility.

For practitioners it's a little bit tougher to avoid staring only at that horizon, because we don't have anyone reminding us to look at how far we have come since we set sail. Since we're in business for ourselves, we need to come up with more creative ways to measure progress in reality. The following are two strategies I use.

Gratitude

Focus on the positive and look for what is going well. I do this by regularly reviewing my progress and allowing myself to feel good about my accomplishments. This daily, weekly, and monthly gratitude exercise allows me to maintain a positive focus, which keeps me from falling into the gap. Sound too simple? Your attitude directly affects what you see. In *The Luck Factor*, Richard Wiseman describes a study he conducted in which each of the participants was given an identical newspaper to look through. They were told to go through the newspaper, count how many pictures there were, and then hand it in to the supervisor. Some people did exactly as asked, spending an average of two minutes on the task. Others, however—the people who self-identified as "lucky"—handed it in almost immediately. Why?

As it turns out, the second page of the newspaper contained a half-page message in two-inch type that said, "Stop counting, there are 43 photos in this newspaper." The "lucky" people saw it straight away, but the "unlucky" people missed it. There was also, halfway through the newspaper, a message of similar size that said, "Stop counting, tell the experimenter you have seen this and win $250." Again, the "unlucky" people were somehow not able to see the message and skipped right past it as they continued to count the pictures.

The study was about positive focus. Pessimists tend not to see all the opportunities in life, whereas optimists see opportunities in everything.

We talked about this in the very first chapter of the book: it starts with attitude. Your thoughts and what you focus on create your reality. Where the mind goes, the qi follows. If your mind-set is "I'm undeserving," "I am not good enough," or some variation thereof, you're effectively telling your patients to stay away. You're missing out on opportunities because of where you put your focus or fail to focus.

There was another study in which researchers had a group of pessimists spend twenty-one days writing down three things they were grateful for every single day. By the end of those three weeks, not only did the pessimists have a better outlook and experience of life, but through PET scans they saw the structure of the brain had actually changed—their synapses had formed new pathways that literally reprogrammed their brains to have a better outlook on life. They were converted, at least in some measure, from pessimism to optimism—just by spending three weeks writing down the things they were grateful for.

So the first thing I do in the morning is I take five minutes to review the last day and write down three things I'm grateful for. It sets my focus for the day and gets my brain to a good place, independent of where I might naturally go when I'm stressed or not feeling good. Take it from me: Like many overachievers, I'm insecure and constantly overcompensating for my insecurity. I get anxious and fearful, too. But I have found that this gratitude meditation protects my confidence and attracts more success in my life, plus it sets the perfect context for the day.

It also helps me measure where I am. It reminds me that "Oh yeah, I got that article published in that paper yesterday, that's really good progress toward my professional goals," or "That patient really has come a long way; I can see how much better a practitioner I am now than I used to be."

Goals

Have you noticed when you are shopping for a new car that the same color and model shows up everywhere? The moment you decide "white Honda Civic," you see them everywhere: at the grocery store, on the street where you live, at the local movie theater; it even happens to be the only car on the lonely road bordering your favorite wilderness location. What's happened? Did everyone around you start buying white Honda Civics?

Of course not. Those cars were always there, you just never noticed before. But now your mind is filtering for them. You're telling your subconscious what to bring to your conscious awareness.

The point here is that *what you focus on becomes your reality.* This is the law of attraction at work. It's your subconscious, and the universe, conspiring to help you achieve that goal.

With that in mind, it's important as you create your goals to make them as real as possible. This means not only visualizing them, but allowing yourself to feel as though you have already achieved them. The subconscious can't tell the difference between now and the future, and emotions are the charge behind the thought. So if you act and behave as if you have that goal now, and really stand in the emotion behind it, your excitement will produce that result far better than if you make the plan without generating that excitement.

When I write down three goals I want to achieve over the next year, I initially don't worry about the how, because this is the dreaming phase where anything is possible and I am programming my subconscious with the final destination. I do think about what it will feel like to have achieved my goals as if a year has already passed. I'm not working myself up, wondering how I'm going to get there. In my mind, it's actually happened. There's no stress. It feels good. So when I do this exercise properly, it *releases* tension, rather than creating it. It should be almost like a relaxing exhale, because in your mind it's already happened.

The use of proper goal setting provides clarity and confidence. And we have to protect our confidence. The more you have a clear vision of where you want to end up, the more you feel like you can really achieve it, the calmer you'll be, and the greater the chance you're going to arrive there. So it's important to allow yourself to imagine, to dream, so you can feel the pleasure of this achievement on a cellular level. You're changing your brain: where the mind goes, the qi follows.

≈ PUT IT INTO PRACTICE ≈

It is worth repeating, the positive focus exercise (also called a gratitude exercise and "what is going well" exercise) will help protect your confidence and keep you out of the gap.

The key to goal setting is to believe it on a cellular level. Hence, visualization is not enough. *You need to feel it.* It is the emotions that power your thoughts. To believe it, you have to feel as if you have already succeeded.

If you do nothing else, use this goal setting process to generate your success for the year:

1. First, get yourself in a positive state by writing three things you're grateful for—don't just review them in your mind, actually write them down. Look for anything that is going well in your life. It can be a small thing like, "I am grateful it rains where I live in Vancouver, as the rain keeps the air quality excellent by pushing the pollution from the air to the ground and roads." Whatever it is, take a moment to really allow yourself to feel the gratitude. The key is in taking the time to allow yourself to *feel* grateful. Repeat this for all three things.

2. Once you are in a more positive state, create three goals for the next year. Make sure they're specific and measurable. Take a moment to visualize what each will look, sound, and feel like when you've accomplished it. Remember, this is dreaming time, so anything is possible. Emotions are the power behind your thoughts, so allow the excitement to seep in when you are visualizing yourself enjoying what you want in life. Every single day, review those goals and act as if you have already achieved them.

It is amazing how this simple process can attract success to your life.

17
De Qi:
Achieving Success

*In life, you're either moving forward
or backward, toward something or
away from it, growing stronger or
becoming weaker. Always strive to
be in a constant positive motion.*

—Michael Irwin

In the first chapter we discussed attitude and the law of attraction. Some people wonder if it actually works; they think that "wishful thinking" never really accomplishes anything. I believe you know otherwise if you have read the chapters leading up to here. This "wishful thinking" can be the most powerful tool in your arsenal, but action must accompany thoughts for them to manifest.

The actions that will lead you to be successful are so simple, they're at risk for being dismissed, but it's important to realize that small actions done regularly over a long period of time have an extraordinary effect. The repetition of those actions over time becomes your successful habit.

That's why it's so important to lay the groundwork we have throughout this book. For each of the actions listed below, remember all of the philosophy and reasons behind them— hopefully those philosophies will motivate you to apply these strategies not just once, but consistently. Anyone can start a marathon, but not everyone can finish. Being successful is simple but not easy.

So with that in mind, here are your action steps to achieve great success.

Daily Actions

- **Gratitude exercise**—Every morning when you first wake up, do the gratitude exercise from the last chapter—write three things you're happy about in your life. This sets the filter to attract more positive things into your life and helps keep you out of the gap.
- **Review goals**—Yes, you want to do this daily. We're so bombarded by information in this world that if we don't, we'll quickly lose sight of what we're really committed to. Reviewing your goals every day helps you maintain that laser focus to get you where you want to go. Make sure you're continuing to visualize the result, and feel as though your goal has already been achieved.
- **Social media**—Carve out a *small* window of time each day to review your various pages and feeds and engage with your audience. Key word here: *small*. Like, 15-30 minutes. Social media is a rabbit hole that's terribly

easy to fall down. Schedule it in, time yourself, and then when the time is done, stop doing it. If you spend your entire day on social media, you won't accomplish anything else. (Check out the tool Hootsuite for scheduling social media posts.)

- **Report of findings for every patient**—One of the best ways to educate each of your patients is detailing how you can help them. You patients are not mind readers, so please communicate on paper your treatment approach and its duration to help them achieve their health goals. Reiterate their health goals so that they know you have heard them. Make it look professional. Include the frequency of treatments and when you plan to reassess.

- **Ask for referrals and testimonials**—When patients compliment you and your treatment, use this as a signal to ask them for a referral or a testimonial. Tell them you'd love to fill your practice with more great people just like them. Never pass up these kinds of opportunities to ask for referrals or testimonials to share on your website and marketing materials.

Weekly Actions

- **Write**—Try to publish one blog post (or other published article) per week to keep your audience interested. Keep it patient centered. This is a great way to maintain mind share, and more importantly to build your credibility as a resource and an authority.

- **Reactivate patients**—Many times, patients leave a visit planning to rebook, and then they forget. Or they want to ponder something, and then never really make a decision. If you let them go too long, they'll often move on. So on a weekly basis, look through your client roster for (1) patients who are in the middle of treatment but don't have another visit scheduled, and (2) people who came in for an initial consult but haven't booked anything. Make a call to those people to check in, see how they're doing, and, if appropriate, either remind them to book their next appointment or invite them to book another one. This isn't about making a hard sale—more often than not, people just forgot because they were busy, and they appreciate the reminder call.
- **Letters to doctors**—Keep building those relationships. Perseverance and patience are key. Send a letter to your patients' medical doctors and any other care provider they may be seeing. Introduce yourself and communicate why your mutual patient is seeing you and that you will communicate with them about any progress within the next three months. This letter serves the following purposes:

  Patient-centered care. Patients value integration and appreciate a team approach. Some doctors will be receptive and correspond with you, which is in the best interest of the patient.

Creates a referral relationship in a non-salesy way. It allows you to meet new medical practitioners and to remind them of you when you send follow-up letters or see another one of their patients, which will often develop into them referring you patients down the road.

- **Continuing education**—Reading a practice-related journal or taking an online course or an in-person workshop that inspires you will boost your confidence (which magnifies the intention you put out into the ether) and attract patients to your practice.

- **Lunch meetings with referral sources**—Set up one lunch meeting per week with either a current referral source or with someone you would like to develop a referral relationship with. This is part of the networking process, to deepen relationships and help keep you fresh in their minds. Depending on how skilled you are at setting up these meetings, you may receive one yes for every ten rejections. Do not get discouraged. You will receive lots of rejections, so remember, persistence is key and continue to "knock on doors" until you have your one weekly meeting. And circle back to those who rejected you in two to three months' time.

Monthly Actions

- **Newsletter**—This is another way to maintain mind share and educate your patients on the benefits of your practice. *Make sure you are creating value.* Remember to think patient-centric and not company-centric. Talk about what you've learned in one of your continual learning courses, a book you've read, a new treatment you've researched that is beneficial to them. List any events that are coming up that they may want to attend. People love recipes, so include a healthy recipe. The point is to create mind share and value for them. If it has no value (it is all about you and not about them), they will unsubscribe or choose to just delete it without reading it thoroughly. *And remember the call to action!*

- **Public talks**—Schedule at least six per year.
- **Acupuncture happy hour**—Offer these in your clinic or community centers once per month.
- **Reevaluations**—Make sure you're helping patients stay out of the gap by showing them how much they've improved.
- **Review and update goals**—I can't emphasize enough how necessary it is that you create clearly defined goals. Clarify, fine-tune, or outright change your goals if they aren't working. This process is organic, so your goals will change as your needs will change.
- **Connect with current referral sources**—Make sure to keep up to date with the people who are sending you referrals; otherwise, out of sight, out of mind. Drug companies have mastered this by having their reps visit doctors on a monthly basis.
- **Press releases**—Send these once per quarter, or as relevance requires.

• **Reactivate patients**—Remember, market first to your best clients. Send an e-mail to any patients you have not seen in over three months to check in with them. How are they doing? Let them know about new offerings, a new skill you developed from a workshop that you know will benefit them, acupuncture happy hour, or an upcoming talk/event. We do this at three months and at six months, and we have patients who say, "Thanks, I'm doing great," and others who say, "Oh, yeah, I forgot about you guys. I'd like to book." Again, this is not a hard sale, it's just creating mind share.

By creating a schedule of these marketing strategies and other actions, you'll be making the law of attraction work for you: your goals are staying front of mind, your actions line up with your goals, and you're accomplishing more, too. Remember, where the mind goes, the qi follows. And so will your practice.

✐ PUT IT INTO PRACTICE ✐

It's time to schedule your daily, weekly, and monthly actions. Set up your calendar to send alerts, and create a daily schedule that starts with the vital gratitude exercise and reviewing your goals.

Conclusion
The World Needs More Rich Acupuncturists

*Choose a job you love, and you'll never
have to work a day in your life.*
— Anonymous

I hope this book has inspired you to take action to help you become more successful. As I said, the action steps to being successful are so simple, they're at risk of being dismissed, but I want you to have that success—the seed to which begins with a positive attitude toward money. As long as you believe money is evil, then you will continue to sabotage yourself. Remember, money is not evil, it is just qi, and it is a reward you receive for providing value and healing others.

The world needs healing, and we need the right people to have the wealth to help heal the world. And I can't think of any better person than an acupuncturist to accomplish that. You have a skill set that makes a difference in the world, but people will not just fall into your lap. It's your responsibility to get yourself out there and create awareness, both of your service and yourself, and if you create value, people will happily pay for your services.

Protect your confidence at all costs. Keep a positive attitude. Keep learning and investing in yourself. Strive to create value. Develop your entrepreneurial skills. Keep sailing toward your horizon, but always take the time to look behind you to see how far you have come along on your journey.

Remember, like it or not, you are a small-business owner. Patients cannot tell the difference between a good acupuncture prescription and a poor one, so also invest in your business skills so that you can reach more people with your healing medicine.

If you enjoyed this book and think a colleague of yours would benefit from reading it too, then please pay it forward and share your copy with a friend or colleague.

The Top Ten Business and Attitude Success Guides for Acupuncturists

1. *The Happiness Advantage: The Seven Principles of Positive Psychology That Fuel Success and Performance at Work* by Shawn Achor

2. *Start with Why: How Great Leaders Inspire Everyone to Take Action* by Simon Sinek

3. *The Compound Effect: Jumpstart Your Income, Your Life, Your Success* by Darren Hardy

4. *Think & Grow Rich* by Napoleon Hill

5. *The 7 Habits of Highly Effective People: Powerful Lessons in Positive Change* by Stephen Covey

6. *The Team Success Handbook: 12 Strategies for Highly Productive Entrepreneurial Teams* by Shannon Waller

7. www.strategiccoach.com

8. *Good to Great: Why Some Companies Make the Leap... and Others Don't* by Jim Collins

9. *Drive: The Surprising Truth about What Motivates Us* by Daniel Pink

10. *The Richest Man in Babylon* by George Samuel Clason

Dr. Lorne Brown is the founder and clinical director of Acubalance Wellness Centre, Pro D Seminars, Medigogy, and the Integrative Fertility Symposium. After a career as a chartered professional accountant (CPA), Lorne received his doctoral degree of traditional Chinese medicine at Vancouver's International College of Traditional Chinese Medicine. Lorne has extensive postgraduate training in gynecology, obstetrics, and reproductive medicine. In 2012, Lorne published the *Acubalance Fertility Diet,* which is made available for free through the Acubalance website.

Internationally known for his pioneering work as an educator and advocate for integrated fertility care, Lorne was the first Canadian to be a certified fellow of the American Board of Oriental Reproductive Medicine (ABORM).

Lorne has presented at fertility conferences and meetings throughout North America, including the 2012 annual meeting of the Canadian Fertility and Andrology Society, the Society of Obstetricians and Gynecologists of Canada (SOCG), and the Science Advisory Panel of Assisted Human Reproduction Canada (AHRC). He participates on numerous other boards and advisory panels as well, including the Quality Assurance Board of the British Columbia College of Traditional Chinese Medicine & Acupuncture (CTCMA), Traditional Chinese Medicine (TCM) Program Advisory Committee for Kwantlen Polytechnic University, and the PDA Advisory Panel for the National Certification Commission for Acupuncture and Oriental Medicine (NCCAOM). Dr. Brown is the acupuncturist advisor to IVF.ca: Canada's premier online fertility community.

Dr. Brown has successfully integrated his entrepreneurial skills and background as a CPA with his passion for Chinese medicine, establishing a very successful fertility practice (Acubalance.ca) and pioneering online continuing education through Pro D Seminars and Medigogy.com for the continued success of Chinese medicine practitioners worldwide.

The latest addition to his bucket list is organizing the International Integrative Fertility Symposium in beautiful Vancouver, British Columbia, where he resides.

This is the best practice advice I've seen; I wish I could have read it years ago! Concise, clear thinking on how to cultivate and harmonize "green energy" in your practice.

—CLAUDIA CITKOVITZ, PhD, LAc

Lorne Brown has mastered the business of Chinese medicine. He practices what he preaches, and his passion for creating a thriving, rewarding medical practice is infectious. Insightful, entertaining, and practical, *Missing the Point* shows you how to bring this ancient art into abundant success in the modern world.

—RANDINE LEWIS, LAc, PhD
Author of *The Infertility Cure*

While most acupuncture schools teach their students to practice Chinese medicine well and to be compassionate and dedicated healers, few offer any in-depth training in how to create and maintain a viable business. For most acupuncturists, myself included, it's learn as you go with many challenges along the way. Lorne Brown's book offers a treasure trove of invaluable clues, hints, and shortcuts on how to handle the business side of our lives with spirit, integrity, joy, and financial success. We are fortunate that Lorne is sharing his well-tested business strategies and wisdom so that we can learn to take care of ourselves as well as our patients!

—LORIE DECHAR
Author of *Five Spirits*

Absolutely recommended reading—Lorne shares practical advice on building a successful career from those starting out to experienced practitioners. This easy-to-read book summarizes several concepts I personally have found invaluable and attribute not only to clinical practice but also to the completion of a textbook. As Lorne discusses in his introduction, it's an incredible medicine we practice, but unfortunately for many it becomes a financial struggle. I can only applaud Lorne's efforts to assist practitioners through sharing his experience in building and maintaining a sustainable career in Chinese medicine.

—Debra Betts, PhD
Author of *Acupuncture in Pregnancy and Birth*

Lorne Brown's book, *Missing the Point*, serves as a wealth-worthiness self-help guide, a best-practices protocol manual, and an introduction to business skills for practicing acupuncturists. All three are desperately needed by those who admirably strive to build our profession while generating right livelihood for themselves. Lorne has the clinical experience and business success to back up what he says. I agree with his opening suggestion that you read this book several times. More important, do what he suggests. It will make a substantial difference in the value you and your patients gain by your practice.

—Felice Dunas, PhD
Author of *Passion Play*

This engaging book distills Lorne's broad personal experience into a number of simple strategies for business success—there is some pertinent advice here for everyone, whether you're just starting out as a new TCM doctor or have spent years working at the clinical coalface. Lorne's legendary drive and enthusiasm come bubbling off the page—he is himself proof of the pudding.

—JANE LYTTLETON
Author of *Treating Infertility with Chinese Medicine*

Lorne's book is an action-oriented and easy read that reminds us that a successful business begins in the mind. He clearly lays out how to develop the skills needed for success, all the while pointing out how limiting beliefs prevent us from having what we want and deserve. Well worth your time, as this book will impact not only your business but also any other aspect of your life that needs a change in mindset.

—YVONNE FARRELL, LAc

Lorne's long experience as both an entrepreneur and health practitioner has informed his book, *Missing the Point*. He helps the practitioner identify and work to expose and thereby evaporate limiting attitudes so that he or she can create the practice they want—whether that is volunteering for MoxAfrica, doing Community Acupuncture, or having a buzzing lucrative urban practice.

—SHARON WEIZENBAUM, LAc
Whitepine Institute